2.06

SODIUM

A TRUE BOOK®
by
Salvatore Tocci

Children's Press®
A Division of Scholastic Inc.

New York Toronto London Auckland Sydney
Mexico City New Delhi Hong Kong
Danbury, Connecticut

Sodium is used to produce the yellow color given off by fireworks.

Reading Consultant
Julia McKenzie Munemo, MEd
New York, New York

Science Consultant
John A. Benner
Austin, Texas

The photo on the cover shows piles of salt. The photo on the title page shows piles of salt at a salt mine.

The author and the publisher are not responsible for injuries or accidents that occur during or from any experiments. Experiments should be conducted in the presence of or with the help of an adult. Any instructions of the experiments that require the use of sharp, hot, or other unsafe items should be conducted by or with the help of an adult.

Library of Congress Cataloging-in-Publication Data

Tocci, Salvatore.
    Sodium / by Salvatore Tocci.
        p. cm. — (A true book)
    Includes bibliographical references and index.
      ISBN 0-516-23702-0 (lib. bdg.)   0-516-25578-9 (pbk.)
      1. Sodium—Juvenile literature. I. Title. II. Series.
QD181.N2T63 2005
      546'.382—dc22   2004027152

CHILDREN'S PRESS, and A TRUE BOOK™, and associated logos are trademarks and/or registered trademarks of Scholastic Library Publishing. SCHOLASTIC and associated logos are trademarks and/or registered trademarks of Scholastic Inc.
1 2 3 4 5 6 7 8 9 10 R 14 13 12 11 10 09 08 07 06 05

Contents

A girl discovers a starfish and shows it to her little brother.

What Have You Discovered?

Have you ever discovered something? Perhaps you were walking one day and you discovered some money lying on the ground. Or you may have discovered something that you thought you had lost, such as your favorite book. You may have even discovered a new friend when you started school this year. If you think about it, you have probably made a lot of discoveries.

Humphry Davy was another person who made a lot of discoveries. Davy was born on December 17, 1778, in England. As a young boy, he loved to explore nature. Then, when he was nineteen years old, Davy read a book about

chemistry that sparked his interest. Chemistry is the study of **matter**, which is the stuff or material that makes up everything in the universe. This book, the chair you are sitting on, and even your body are all made of matter.

Matter exists as solids, liquids, and gases. Davy's first discoveries came from his study of gases. He worked with one that is commonly known as laughing gas.

Humphry Davy became seriously ill in 1827 and died in 1829. Some people suspect that his illness was caused by all the gases he inhaled over the years.

Davy frequently spoke about his work to the public. He would often breathe in the gas that he was discussing to show his audience how it affected the human body. In the case of laughing gas, he once breathed in 16 quarts (15 liters) in just seven minutes. All this laughing gas made him quite light-headed and dizzy.

Davy went on to study the effects of passing electricity through various solids that he melted into liquids. He discovered that electricity broke apart these liquids into simpler substances. These simpler substances are known as **elements**. An element is one of the building blocks of matter. From his experiments with electricity, Davy discovered several elements. One of the first elements he discovered was sodium. He discovered it in 1807.

What Is Sodium?

Every element has both a name and a symbol. The symbol for sodium is Na. This symbol comes from the first two letters of the Latin word *natrium*, which is the word the ancient Romans used for a substance called soda ash.

Davy discovered sodium by passing electricity through soda ash. He named the new element he discovered sodium, based on the word *soda*.

Like most other elements, sodium is a metal. A metal is a substance that is a **conductor** of electricity. You may think that all metals, such as gold and copper, are hard and shiny. Some metals, however, are soft and dull. Sodium is one such metal. It is so soft that it can

Gloves should be worn when handling sodium because it can damage the skin.

be cut with a plastic knife. Sodium also tarnishes to a dull, grayish color when it is exposed to the air.

These men are mining salt, a sodium compound, from a salt mine in the Dominican Republic.

As the sixth most abundant element on Earth, sodium can be found almost anywhere in nature. Pure sodium, however, does not exist in nature because it is a very active element. In other words, sodium reacts with almost anything it comes into contact with, including other elements, the air, and water.

Sodium is so active that an explosion occurs when it comes in contact with the element chlorine. Chlorine is a poisonous gas. When these two elements are mixed, a violent reaction occurs. When everything settles down, all that is left is a substance that is neither reactive nor poisonous. Scientists call this substance sodium chloride. You call it table salt.

Table salt contains sodium.

Salting Ice

Salt is sprinkled on roads in winter to melt the ice. Find out why salt causes the ice to melt. Ask an adult to wrap a towel around some ice cubes and use a hammer to crush them. Place the crushed ice in a glass or cup. Insert a thermometer into the ice. Wait a few minutes and then look at the temperature. Add 2 teaspoons of salt to the ice and stir. Watch what happens to the temperature. Adding salt lowers the temperature.

Why Do We Need Salt?

Sodium chloride is a **compound**, which is a substance that is made up of the combination of two or more elements. There are millions of different kinds of compounds. In fact, there are many kinds of salts besides sodium chloride. All of these compounds, however, are made up of just a few more than one hundred different elements.

How can so many different kinds of compounds be made from so few elements? Think about the English language. Just twenty-six letters can be arranged to make up all the words in the English language. Likewise, the one hundred different elements can be arranged to make up all the different kinds of compounds that exist.

The fluids in our bodies are just slightly less than 1 percent sodium chloride. These fluids include blood, sweat, and tears. If sweat or tears have ever accidentally gotten into your mouth, then you know that they taste salty. Inside our bodies, the sodium from salt plays several important roles.

Nerves need sodium to function normally. Without sodium, nerves would not be able to send information to different

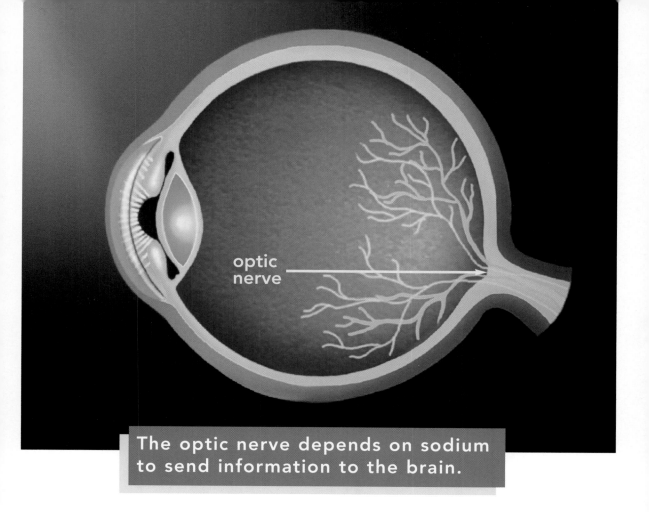

optic
nerve

The optic nerve depends on sodium to send information to the brain.

parts of the body. For example, a large nerve at the back of the eye transmits information to the brain. The brain then interprets this information as the images a person sees. Without sodium, this nerve would not be able to send information to the brain. As a result, a person would not see anything.

Muscles also depend on sodium to function normally. Nerves control muscles that are attached to bones. These nerves cause the muscles to contract. As the muscles contract, they move the bones. Without sodium, nerves would not be able to cause the muscles to contract. As a result, a person would not be able to move parts of the body, such as the head, arms, or legs.

The body needs salt to maintain the level of sodium in body fluids. Anyone who sweats a lot because of exercise or hot weather can lose too much body fluid and become dehydrated. This person is losing not only water but also sodium. In

Some athletes take salt tablets to replace the sodium they lose through sweating.

addition to drinking liquids, the person must take in enough sodium to replace what has been lost through sweat. If the sodium is not replaced, the person may develop severe muscle cramps.

Most people get the sodium they need from the salt in their diets. Foods that are processed, such as canned and preserved products, contain more than enough salt for the body's needs. People who eat a lot of these foods or who add a lot of table salt to the foods they eat may take

To help keep your body healthy, it is best to eat only small amounts of salty foods like these.

in too much sodium. A diet high in sodium is one cause of high blood pressure.

How Else Is Sodium Useful?

Sodium has limited uses because it is such an active metal. One place that it has been put to use is in street-lights known as sodium **vapor** lamps. A clear plastic tube is filled with the vapor, which is commonly called gas. Even as

Sodium vapor lamps are very efficient in turning electricity into light.

a gas, sodium conducts electricity well. Electricity is passed through the sodium vapor, which turns the electricity into light. The light given off by sodium vapor lamps has an orange-yellow color.

Sodium vapor lamps are used for street lighting, parking lot lighting, and car lighting for several reasons. Their yellowish color is similar to the color given off by caution lights, and therefore it is likely to make drivers be a little more careful on the road. This yellowish light can also penetrate fog. The light from sodium vapor lamps is also soft and not glaring. For this reason, these lights were chosen to light up San Francisco's Golden Gate Bridge when it opened in 1937.

Sodium vapor lamps have also helped astronomers study the night sky. Other light sources produce a bright light that sets the sky aglow. This bright light

The Golden Gate Bridge is one of the longest suspension bridges in the world.

makes it difficult to study dim objects in the night sky. Scientists call this "light pollution."

At one time, San Diego, California, required that only sodium vapor lamps be used on city streets. This step was taken to help reduce light pollution that was interfering with the work of astronomers at a nearby university. Today, that law is no longer in effect. Someday, astronomers may have to work far from cities that do not use sodium vapor lamps.

The tube in this light bulb is made of a special glass
that can contain sodium vapor at high temperatures.

Because sodium is so active, it forms many different compounds with other elements. Many of these sodium compounds are very useful and can be found in many homes.

One such compound is sodium carbonate, which is commonly known as soda ash. This is the compound that Davy used to isolate pure sodium. Today, sodium carbonate is used to make glass and paper. It is also used in water softeners.

Washing with soap and shampoo in soft water gets the skin and hair cleaner.

Another useful compound is sodium bicarbonate, which is commonly known as baking soda.

Baking soda is made from soda ash. It can be used for many tasks besides baking.

If you check the label on a box of baking soda, you will see how many uses it has in the home. This sodium compound can be used to clean almost everything in the house, wash clothes, absorb odors, and soothe tired feet.

As its name suggests, the main use of baking soda is for baking. Baking soda is often added to bread dough and cake batter. As it is heated in the oven, baking soda

Without sodium bicarbonate, this cake would not rise while being baked.

produces a gas called carbon dioxide. This gas causes the bread or cake to rise.

Making It Pop

Try this experiment outside. If you have to work inside, use a sink or bathtub. Test a plastic zipper-lock bag to make sure it does not leak. Pour about 4 ounces (about 120 milliliters) of water into it, seal it shut, and turn it upside down. If it does not leak, pour out the water. Add 4 ounces (about 120ml) of vinegar and 2 ounces (about 60ml) of warm water to the bag. Place 2 table-spoons of baking soda in a paper napkin.

Fold the napkin and place it inside the bag. Quickly seal the bag. Shake it gently and drop the bag on the ground or into the sink. The carbon dioxide gas that is created should inflate the bag and cause it to pop open. Experiment to see how you can make the bag pop the fastest. Try different bag sizes and vary how much vinegar, water, and baking soda you add. Does cold water work just as well as warm water?

A woman pours drain cleaner down a sink drain to try to break up a clog. Drain cleaners contain sodium hydroxide.

Another useful sodium compound is found under many kitchen or bathroom sinks.

This compound is sodium hydroxide, and it is the main ingredient in drain cleaners. Sodium hydroxide is commonly called lye. Lye reacts with the grease that can clog drains. Lye and grease combine to form soap, which washes down the drain easily.

When Humphry Davy discovered sodium, he had no idea how useful it would turn out to be. So keep looking for new discoveries. You never know what you'll find.

Fun Facts About Sodium

- To produce enough electricity to isolate sodium from soda ash, Davy built a battery that was about the size of a small room.

- Pure sodium must be stored in a special liquid, such as kerosene, to prevent it from reacting with the air or water.

- Sodium vapor lamps were first used to illuminate a highway in Europe in 1933.

- When people are being questioned, the "truth serum" that is used to make them talk more is a sodium compound.

- The preservative that is added to hot dogs is a sodium compound.

- A quarter-pound cheeseburger, large fries, and 16-ounce (0.5 liter) soda will supply almost three times the amount of sodium an adult needs each day to stay healthy.

- Sodium is used to produce the yellow color given off by fireworks.

To Find Out More

To learn more about sodium, check out these additional sources.

Books

Blashfield, Jean F. **Sodium.** Raintree/Steck Vaughn, 1998.

O'Daly, Anne. **Sodium.** Benchmark Books, 2001.

Saunders, Nigel. **Sodium and the Alkali Metals.** Heinemann Library, 2004.

Tocci, Salvatore. **The Periodic Table.** Children's Press. 2004.

Bridge Light
http://www.exploratorium. edu/snacks/bridge_light.html

Experiment with two pieces of clear plastic and light, including the light from a sodium vapor lamp (a yellow streetlight).

Choose a Diet Moderate in Salt and Sodium
http://www.nal.usda.gov/fnic /dga/dga95/sodium.html

One of the interesting things you can learn on this site is how you can get all the sodium you need from just 1 teaspoon of table salt. Suggestions for eating a diet that is low in sodium are given.

Fizzing and Foaming
http://scifun.chem.wisc. edu/HOMEEXPTS/ FIZZFOAM.html

Use the juice from red cabbage or grape juice to see changes in color when you add vinegar to baking soda in water.

The Great Sodium Disaster
http://www.allatoms.com/ SodiumWaterExpt/NaExp. htm

Dropping sodium into water is very dangerous. You can safely see what happens when these two substances react at this site. It has photographs showing advanced chemistry students carrying out this experiment under their teacher's supervision. One photograph shows the explosion that occurs.

Salt in Water Softening
http://www.saltinfo.com/ water%20softening.htm

Learn how sodium is used to soften water by removing two other elements that make it hard.

Important Words

chemistry study of matter and how it changes

compound substance formed when two or more elements are combined

conductor substance through which electricity and heat pass

element building block of matter

matter stuff or material that makes up everything in the universe

vapor gas

Index

Meet the Author

Salvatore Tocci is a science writer who lives in East Hampton, New York, with his wife, Patti. He was a high school biology and chemistry teacher for almost thirty years. His books include a high school chemistry textbook and an elementary school book series that encourages students to perform experiments to learn about science. As a chemistry teacher, he demonstrated to his students what happens when a very small piece of sodium is dropped into water.